ALTO SAX

S0-AHF-655

Movie Music

HOW TO USE THE CD ACCOMPANIMENT:
A MELODY CUE APPEARS ON THE RIGHT CHANNEL ONLY. IF YOUR
CD PLAYER HAS A BALANCE ADJUSTMENT, YOU CAN ADJUST THE
VOLUME OF THE MELODY BY TURNING DOWN THE RIGHT CHANNEL.

ISBN 0-634-08368-6

HAL•LEONARD®
CORPORATION
7777 W. BLUEMOUND RD. P.O. BOX 13819 MILWAUKEE, WI 53213

Visit Hal Leonard Online at
www.halleonard.com

◆ AND ALL THAT JAZZ

from CHICAGO

ALTO SAX

Words by FRED EBB
Music by JOHN KANDER

3

That jazz!

② BELIEVE

from Warner Bros. Pictures' THE POLAR EXPRESS

ALTO SAX

Words and Music by GLEN BALLARD
and ALAN SILVESTRI

❸ BEYOND THE SEA

featured in the Walt Disney/Pixar film FINDING NEMO

ALTO SAX

Words and Music by CHARLES TRENET,
ALBERT LASRY and JACK LAWRENCE

◆ BREAKAWAY

from THE PRINCESS DIARIES 2: ROYAL ENGAGEMENT

ALTO SAX

Words and Music by BRIDGET BENENATE,
AVRIL LAVIGNE and MATTHEW GERRARD

⑤ COME WHAT MAY

from the Motion Picture MOULIN ROUGE

ALTO SAX

Words and Music by
DAVID BAERWALD

GEORGIA ON MY MIND

from RAY

ALTO SAX

Words by STUART GORRELL
Music by HOAGY CARMICHAEL

7 I AM A MAN OF CONSTANT SORROW

featured in O BROTHER, WHERE ART THOU?

ALTO SAX

Words and Music by
CARTER STANLEY

◆8 I BELIEVE I CAN FLY

from SPACE JAM

ALTO SAX

Words and Music by
ROBERT KELLY

◆⑨ I WALK THE LINE

from WALK THE LINE

ALTO SAX

Words and Music by
JOHN R. CASH

LEARN TO BE LONELY

from THE PHANTOM OF THE OPERA

ALTO SAX

Music by ANDREW LLOYD WEBBER
Lyrics by CHARLES HART

THE INCREDITS

from Walt Disney Pictures' THE INCREDIBLES - A Pixar Film

ALTO SAX

Music by MICHAEL GIACCHINO